Classidy Hutchinson

Cassidy Hutchinson Biography and the Capitol Attack of January 6

Timeless Talesmith

Table of Content

Introduction

In the annals of American history, certain moments stand out as turning points—moments that shake the very foundations of democracy and reshape the course of a nation. Among these pivotal moments, the events of January 6, 2021, hold a place of profound significance. It was a day when the hallowed halls of the United States Capitol were breached, and the ideals of democracy were put to the test.

At the heart of this historic episode is Cassidy Jacqueline Hutchinson, a name that would soon become synonymous with the tumultuous events of that day. Born in 1996, Cassidy Hutchinson began her journey as an American patriot, dedicated to her nation's ideals and service to its highest office. She rose through the ranks, serving as a former White House aide during the Trump administration, where she held the position of assistant to then-Chief of Staff Mark Meadows.

But it was not her tenure in the White House that would thrust her into the national spotlight. Instead, it was her role as a pivotal witness in one of the most consequential public hearings in recent memory. On June 28, 2022, Cassidy Hutchinson stepped into the glaring spotlight of the United States House Select Committee on the January 6 Attack.

With unwavering resolve and a commitment to truth, Cassidy Hutchinson testified about the conduct of President Donald Trump, his senior aides, and his political allies in the lead-up to and during the fateful January 6 United States Capitol attack. Her words would resound across the nation, captivating audiences and igniting impassioned debates.

In the wake of her testimony, Cassidy Hutchinson's name would be etched into the annals of history. Her compelling and explosive revelations would garner widespread attention, transcending political divides and prompting a national reckoning. Yet, they would also draw the ire of Trump allies, setting the stage for a dramatic and transformative chapter in American politics.

Join us as we delve into the life and times of Cassidy Hutchinson, a witness to history, a voice of truth, and a symbol of resilience in the face of unprecedented challenges. Through her story, we navigate the turbulent waters of the January 6 Capitol attack, exploring the profound impact it had on the nation and the individuals who played pivotal roles on that unforgettable day. Cassidy Hutchinson's journey is a testament to the enduring power of conviction and the enduring quest for accountability in the face of adversity.

Early Life and Education

In the quiet town of Pennington, New Jersey, nestled amidst the lush landscapes and tranquil streets, a young and ambitious Classidy Hutchinson embarked on her journey through life. It was here, in this quaint corner of the Garden State, that her remarkable story began to unfold.

Born and raised in Pennington, Classidy Hutchinson's formative years were imbued with the charm of small-town America. Pennington, with its close-knit community and picturesque surroundings, provided the perfect backdrop for a young girl's dreams to take root and flourish. The streets of Pennington, lined with historic houses and friendly faces, were her playground, and the sense of belonging she felt here would shape her character in profound ways.

As a child, Classidy displayed an insatiable curiosity about the world around her. She was the kind of youngster who would pester her parents with endless questions, eager to unravel the mysteries of life. Her innate inquisitiveness and thirst for knowledge hinted at the potential for greatness that lay within her.

Classidy Hutchinson's educational journey took a significant step forward when she enrolled at Hopewell Valley Central High School. This institution, known for its commitment to academic excellence, became the crucible where her intellectual prowess was forged. It was during these formative years that her passion for politics began to take root.

As a student at Hopewell Valley Central High School, Classidy quickly made a name for herself. She was not just a diligent scholar but also an active participant in extracurricular activities. Her involvement in debate clubs and student government showcased her natural leadership abilities. Even then, those who knew her couldn't help but predict a bright future for this young, determined girl from Pennington.

Upon graduating from high school in 2015, Classidy Hutchinson set her sights on a new horizon: higher education. Her destination? Christopher Newport University. This leap marked the beginning of an exciting chapter in her life.

From 2015 to 2018, Classidy dedicated herself to her studies at Christopher Newport University. The campus, situated in the heart of Newport News, Virginia, was a far cry from the quiet streets of Pennington. It was a vibrant and dynamic place where ideas clashed, and perspectives intermingled. It was precisely the kind of environment that would nurture her passion for political science and American studies.

In 2019, Classidy Hutchinson stood on the cusp of a significant achievement. With grit and determination, she successfully completed her academic journey at Christopher Newport University, earning herself a Bachelor of Arts degree in political science and American studies. Her graduation was not just a personal triumph but a testament to the hard work and dedication that had defined her path.

This achievement was particularly poignant for Classidy because she proudly identified as a "first-generation college student." She carried the hopes and dreams of her family and community on her shoulders, breaking new ground and setting an example for those who would follow in her footsteps. Her story was a testament to the power of education to transform lives and open doors to a brighter future.

In the early chapters of Classidy Hutchinson's life, we find the building blocks of a remarkable journey. From the idyllic streets of Pennington to the hallowed halls of Christopher Newport University, she was shaped by her surroundings and driven by an unwavering commitment to knowledge and progress.

The tale of her early life and education is not just a story of personal achievement but a testament to the resilience and determination that define the American spirit. Classidy Hutchinson's journey had only just begun, but the foundation for greatness had been firmly laid. In the pages that follow, we will delve deeper into her exploits, her challenges, and her unwavering dedication to the world of politics, which would eventually lead her to the center stage of one of America's most pivotal moments.

Entry into Politics

Classidy Hutchinson's journey into the world of politics was nothing short of remarkable. It was during her time at Christopher Newport University that she embarked on a path that would ultimately lead her to the heart of American political power. In this chapter, we delve into the intriguing story of how a young and ambitious student found herself working alongside some of the most influential figures in American politics.

Classidy Hutchinson's story begins on the picturesque campus of Christopher Newport University. Nestled in the heart of Newport News, Virginia, this institution would serve as the launching pad for her political aspirations. But how did it all begin?

During the summer of 2016, while still a student at Christopher Newport University, Classidy secured a coveted internship with none other than Republican Senator Ted Cruz. It was a pivotal moment in her life, one that would set the stage for her future in politics. She found herself in the heart of the political action, working alongside Cruz's dedicated team.

For a young college student, this was an opportunity of a lifetime. The halls of the Senate echoed with debates, and the buzz of political discourse filled the air. Classidy was not merely an observer; she was an active participant in the political process. Her responsibilities ranged from conducting research on key policy issues to assisting with constituent inquiries.

Classidy's internship with Senator Cruz provided her with invaluable insights into the workings of American politics. She was exposed to the intricacies of legislative processes, witnessed the power of persuasion in the Senate chamber, and interacted with senators, staffers, and constituents from all walks of life.

But Classidy Hutchinson was not content to rest on her laurels. She had tasted the world of politics and was hungry for more. The following summer, in 2017, she took on another significant challenge by interning for Republican US House of Representatives whip Steve Scalise. This time, she found herself on Capitol Hill, amidst the iconic domed buildings that symbolized the heart of American democracy.

As an intern for Representative Scalise, Classidy's responsibilities expanded. She worked closely with Scalise's team, aiding in the coordination of legislative initiatives and gaining firsthand experience in the art of whipping votes. It was a demanding role, but Classidy thrived in this high-stakes environment.

With each passing summer, Classidy Hutchinson's political acumen and reputation grew. In 2018, she embarked on yet another thrilling adventure by securing an internship in the White House Office of Legislative Affairs. This was the pinnacle of political internships, a dream come true for any aspiring political strategist.

Within the hallowed halls of the White House, Classidy was exposed to the epicenter of executive power. She worked alongside seasoned professionals who shaped the policies that would impact the nation. The fast-paced environment demanded quick thinking and unwavering dedication, qualities Classidy possessed in abundance.

Her internship at the White House Office of Legislative Affairs was not merely a stepping stone; it was a springboard. Impressed by her dedication and competence, Classidy was offered a full-time position within the office. She had transitioned from being an intern to a valued member of the White House team, a testament to her unwavering commitment to public service.

In March of 2020, Classidy Hutchinson's journey into the world of politics took an unexpected turn. It was a pivotal moment, one that would shape her career and thrust her into the inner circle of power within the Trump administration.

At that time, the Trump administration was no stranger to staff shake-ups. Mark Meadows, a seasoned political operative, was appointed as Trump's fourth chief of staff. With Meadows at the helm, change was in the air, and it was in this climate of transition that Classidy Hutchinson found herself in a position that would change the trajectory of her political career.

Meadows wasted no time in assembling his team, and he saw something promising in Hutchinson. He tapped her to serve as one of his aides, a decision that would prove to be a game-changer for both of them. Little did anyone know that this would be the start of a remarkable journey.

In her new role, Hutchinson quickly rose through the ranks, becoming Meadows' principal assistant. Her responsibilities were far-reaching, and her influence within the White House began to grow. Her official title, "Special Assistant to the President and Coordinator for Legislative Affairs," was a testament to the importance of her role within the administration.

Her office was strategically located, just down the hall from the Oval Office. This proximity to the epicenter of power meant that she was always in the thick of things, where decisions of immense consequence were made. Hutchinson was no mere spectator; she was an active participant in the political drama that unfolded within those hallowed halls.

One of her key duties was to take meticulous notes during high-level meetings. These notes were not mere scribbles on a legal pad; they were a record of history in the making. Hutchinson's attention to detail and her ability to capture the essence of discussions would prove invaluable in the days and months to come.

But her role extended beyond the confines of the West Wing. Hutchinson became a constant companion to Meadows, traveling with him as he crisscrossed the country. She was more than just an aide; she was a trusted advisor, a confidante who was privy to the inner workings of the Trump administration.

It was during these travels that Hutchinson often found herself at the center of attention. Her presence did not go unnoticed, and the media soon took an interest in this rising star of the Trump administration. She was often described as a close confidante of Meadows, a testament to the trust and camaraderie that had developed between them.

One memorable moment that captured the public's imagination occurred during Trump's September 21, 2020, campaign rally in Swanton, Ohio. In a nationally-syndicated AP photograph, Classidy Hutchinson was depicted in a moment of pure joy. She was seen dancing to the infectious beats of the Village People's iconic song "Y.M.C.A." alongside none other than White House press secretary Kayleigh McEnany. The image spoke volumes about Hutchinson's personality - vibrant, energetic, and unapologetically herself.

As Hutchinson's star continued to rise within the Trump administration, she found herself in situations that would challenge her in unexpected ways. In her 2023 memoir titled "Enough," Hutchinson made a shocking revelation. She alleged that Rudy Giuliani, the former mayor of New York City and a prominent figure in Trump's legal team, had groped her backstage during Donald Trump's speech on January 6, 2021. This revelation sent shockwaves through the political world, adding another layer of intrigue to an already tumultuous period in American history.

As Trump's term drew to a close, there were whispers of what the future held for Classidy Hutchinson. Trump himself claimed that she was slated to work for his post-presidency operation in Florida, a role that would have undoubtedly kept her in the spotlight. However, as with many things in politics, plans can change abruptly. Trump's vision for Hutchinson's post-presidential role was, in his own words, "abruptly dropped" before she could step into it.

The reasons for this sudden change remain shrouded in mystery, leaving room for speculation and intrigue. It's a testament to the unpredictable nature of politics, where one moment you can be on the cusp of a new chapter in your career, and the next moment, it all unravels.

Classidy Hutchinson's journey into politics had been nothing short of remarkable. From her humble beginnings as an aide to becoming a trusted advisor in the White House, her story was one of ambition, resilience, and unexpected twists. As the pages of her life continued to turn, one could only wonder what the future held for this enigmatic figure in American politics.

January 6 Event

Attempts to overturn the presidential election

On a crisp and cold winter morning, the United States Capitol stood as a symbol of democracy, where the will of the people was enshrined in every brick and column. It was January 6, 2021, a day that would forever be etched in American history, and a day when the peaceful transfer of power was put to a severe test.

To understand the events of that fateful day, we must rewind to the backdrop of a contentious election. In November 2020, Democrat Joe Biden emerged victorious over incumbent Republican Donald Trump in the presidential race. However, Trump, unwilling to accept defeat, embarked on a mission to overturn the election results. He and other Republicans relentlessly peddled false claims of widespread voter fraud, sowing seeds of doubt and division across the nation.

In the days following the election, Trump took to his favored platform, Twitter, with a tweet that sent shockwaves through the nation. In all caps, he declared, "I WON THIS ELECTION, BY A LOT!" Twitter, in a rare move, added a label cautioning that official sources had not yet called the race. The tweet, timestamped at 10:36 PM on November 7,

2020, marked the beginning of a tumultuous period in American politics.

Trump's tweet shortly after polls had closed

As votes were still being counted and the nation awaited the official results, Trump did something unprecedented. He prematurely declared victory, demanding that the ongoing counting of votes be halted. It was a move that would set the stage for a remarkable and chaotic chapter in American history.

Trump's legal team, in the wake of the election, conducted a swift review and concluded that their claims of election fraud had no factual basis or legal merit. Despite this, Trump launched a barrage of legal challenges, filing no less than sixty lawsuits in an attempt to overturn the results. This included two cases brought before the Supreme Court. The overarching goal was to nullify the election certifications and void votes cast for Joe Biden. The courts, however, repeatedly rejected these claims, citing a lack of evidence or legal standing.

Unfazed by the legal setbacks, Trump embarked on a campaign to pressure Republican officials in key states. He sought to replace slates of Biden electors with those loyal to him, or to manufacture evidence of fraud. He pushed for investigations into election "irregularities," like signature matches on mailed-in ballots, dismissing prior analyses and investigations that found no substantial issues. Trump even floated the idea of invoking martial law to "re-run" or reverse the election, and he considered appointing a special counsel to uncover fraud, despite contrary conclusions from federal and state officials.

One of the most extraordinary aspects of this period was Trump's relentless pressure on Vice President Mike Pence. Trump repeatedly urged Pence to take actions well beyond the scope of his constitutional powers as vice president and president of the Senate. This pressure culminated in a rally speech on the morning of January 6, where Trump implored Pence to stop Biden from taking office.

As this drama unfolded, scholars, historians, political scientists, and journalists began to use stark terms to describe the situation. They characterized Trump's efforts as an attempted self-coup, an endeavor to seize power through undemocratic means. This was the implementation of what would become known as the "big lie," a false narrative that threatened the very foundations of American democracy.

The events of January 6 would have far-reaching consequences. On that dark day, the United States Capitol was breached by a mob of Trump supporters, resulting in chaos, violence, and the tragic loss of lives. The world watched in disbelief as the heart of American democracy came under siege.

In the aftermath, investigations and legal proceedings would ensue, ultimately leading to Donald Trump becoming a target in the Smith special counsel investigation, a momentous development that signaled accountability for those involved in the events of January 6, 2021.

Planning of January 6 events

On December 18, just four days after the Electoral College had cast its votes, former President Donald Trump took to his favorite medium, Twitter, to send a rallying cry to his supporters. "Big protest in D.C. on January 6th. Be there, will be wild!" he tweeted. With those words, the stage was set for a gathering that would captivate the nation and leave an indelible mark on the nation's capital.

The call was out, and Trump's followers responded with fervor. The allure of a "wild" event in the heart of the country's political epicenter was irresistible. But behind the scenes, there was more to this event than met the eye.

As the days counted down to January 6, whispers of collaboration between far-right groups and activists began to surface. Ali Alexander, a prominent figure in far-right circles, didn't mince his words. He described a plan to "build momentum and pressure" leading up to the big day. Their goal? To change the hearts and minds of those in Congress who had not yet made up their minds or were wary of the gathering mob outside the Capitol.

Alexander, a man not known for subtlety, named names. He pointed to three Republican members of the House: Gosar, Biggs, and Brooks, as key players in this grand design. "We're the four guys who came up with a January 6 event," he boldly declared. The intrigue was building as the cast of characters grew.

December 23, 2020, marked a significant turning point. Roger Stone's group, Stop the Steal, posted plans that sent shivers through the nation. They vowed to occupy the Capitol and made it clear that they would "escalate" if met with opposition from law enforcement. It was a declaration of intent that could not be ignored.

By January 1, Roger Stone himself stepped into the spotlight, recording a video for his "Stop The Steal Security Project." In it, he made a plea for funds, funds that would be crucial for staging the event, providing transportation, and, most importantly, ensuring security. The stakes were rising, and the call for support was echoing in the hearts of many.

Every grand event needs a patron, and the January 6 gathering was no exception. Behind the scenes, Julie Jenkins Fancelli, a 72-year-old heiress to the Publix supermarket fortune, played a pivotal role. She was the financial powerhouse, budgeting a staggering $3 million for the event and willingly spending at least $650,000 of her own wealth.

Fancelli's influence extended far beyond her checkbook. Through the channels of conspiracy theorist Alex Jones, her funding secured the reservation of the Ellipse, a prime location for their assembly. With Fancelli's support, a robocall campaign was launched, urging people to "march to the Capitol building and call on Congress to stop the steal." The pieces were falling into place.

Charlie Kirk, another activist supported by Fancelli's generosity, took to social media to announce that his group had dispatched over eighty buses to transport attendees to the Capitol. The event was gaining momentum, and the nation was watching.

And then came the bombshell: Alex Jones claimed that the Trump White House had asked him to lead the march to the Capitol. It was a revelation that left many astonished, as the line between official endorsement and grassroots movement blurred.

On January 2, just days before the event that would rock the nation, former President Trump announced his plans to speak at the "March to Save America" rally scheduled for January 6. This declaration sent shockwaves through the political landscape, solidifying the event's significance.

But Trump wasn't the only one making headlines in the run-up to January 6. On January 4, 2021, Steve Bannon, a former White House advisor, made a startling assertion. He declared himself to be part of what he dubbed "the bloodless coup." The phrase reverberated through the media, igniting debates and speculations about what lay ahead.

Seditious conspiracy by Oath Keepers and Proud Boys

It was the evening of November 5, 2020, just two days after the presidential election that would come to define an era. As the nation held its breath, leaders of the Oath Keepers, a far-right paramilitary group, began exchanging messages that would sow the seeds of a dangerous conspiracy. They whispered about a "civil war," a chilling phrase that sent shivers down the spines of those who stumbled upon their sinister conversations.

By November 9, Oath Keeper leaders had escalated their discussions to a terrifying level. In an online members-only video conference, the group's leader, Stewart Rhodes, meticulously outlined a plan to thwart the peaceful transfer of power. Their method? Unsettlingly, they contemplated the use of force to achieve their ominous goal.

The Oath Keepers weren't content with mere talk; they were making concrete preparations for the storm they believed was coming. Their plan included the establishment of what they ominously called a "Quick Reaction Force" (QRF), complete with an arsenal of weaponry. Their chosen location? The nearby city of Alexandria, Virginia. They even planned to secure boat transportation to ensure that bridge closures wouldn't thwart their entry into the nation's capital.

As December dawned, the web of conspiracy extended its reach. On December 19, Kelly Meggs, a leader of the Oath Keepers, made a fateful call to another far-right group, the Proud Boys, led by Enrique Tarrio. The next day, the Proud Boys leadership handpicked their members to form a new chapter known as the "Ministry of Self Defense." This new entity was given the ominous responsibility of "national rally planning." A foreboding message appeared in their communications: "I am assuming most of the protest will be at the capital [sic] building given what's going on inside."

The Proud Boys, not to be outdone, began rallying their troops for what would become a historic and chaotic day. They turned to crowdfunding to finance their mission and began acquiring paramilitary equipment, including concealed tactical vests and radio gear. The days leading up to January 6 were spent meticulously plotting the impending attack.

On December 29, the Proud Boys' leadership announced their intention to go "incognito" on January 6, deciding not to wear their traditional black and yellow attire. As December turned to January, they received a document titled "1776 Returns," a call to occupy "crucial buildings" on January 6, invoking a disturbing reference to "Storm the Winter Palace," eerily reminiscent of an attack on the Capitol.

As January 3 arrived, Stewart Rhodes left his home in Texas, embarking on a journey that would cost him over $10,000 in firearms equipment alone. He was on his way to Washington, D.C., driven by a dangerous determination to disrupt the democratic process. On January 5, Oath Keeper leaders began unloading their cache of weapons with the QRF in Alexandria, a sign that the storm was drawing nearer.

January 4 brought a significant turn of events as Tarrio, the Proud Boys' leader, was arrested by D.C. police for a prior destruction of property charge. Fearful that the authorities would gain access to Tarrio's messages, the leadership promptly dismantled the old group chat and established a new one. Their chilling confidence was evident as one leader remarked, "Well at least they won't get our boots on the ground plans because we are one step ahead of them." Tarrio's release on January 5 didn't deter him; he met with Stewart Rhodes in an underground parking garage, sealing their pact of insurrection.

The night of January 5 was fraught with tension as Proud Boys leaders mobilized their troops. Members were grouped into teams, issued radios, and instructed on specific communication channels. Their rallying point was set at 10 a.m. – the iconic Washington Monument. Leadership issued stern warnings to avoid the police and abstain from public drinking, as their nefarious plans drew nearer.

Law Enforcement and National Guard preparations

On November 9, 2020, President Trump took a controversial step by firing Secretary of Defense Mark Esper and replacing him with Christopher C. Miller, who assumed the role of acting Secretary. This move sent shockwaves through the defense establishment and raised eyebrows across the nation. It was a clear sign of the President's intent to exert control over key agencies in the final weeks of his term.

In the wake of Esper's firing, Central Intelligence Agency (CIA) Director Gina Haspel confided in Chairman of the Joint Chiefs of Staff Mark Milley, expressing her grave concerns. In a private conversation, she chillingly remarked, "we are on the way to a right-wing coup." This statement, made by a senior intelligence official, underscored the gravity of the situation and set the stage for the events to come.

As January 6 approached, alarm bells were ringing in Washington. Senator Mitt Romney, a prominent Republican, reached out to Senate Majority Leader Mitch McConnell with a foreboding message. In a letter, Romney revealed disturbing intelligence reports about planned protests on that fateful day. He wrote, "...a senior official at the Pentagon... reports that they are seeing very disturbing social media traffic regarding the protests planned on the 6th. There are calls to burn down your home, Mitch;

to smuggle guns into DC, and to storm the Capitol." Romney's letter highlighted the potential for violence and raised doubts about whether sufficient security measures were in place.

On January 3, 2021, a remarkable event took place. All ten living former defense secretaries released an open letter expressing their deep concerns about the possibility of a military coup to overturn the election results. In a rare move, they named the recently-appointed Acting Secretary of Defense, Christopher Miller, in their letter. Their collective voice added weight to the growing unease about the situation.

The day after this extraordinary letter was made public, President Trump issued a directive to Christopher Miller, instructing him to take action to "protect the demonstrators" on January 6. This directive, coming from the Commander-in-Chief, was viewed with a mixture of apprehension and confusion. It signaled a potentially volatile situation.

Christopher Miller wasted no time in implementing Trump's directive. On January 4, he signed a memo that severely restricted the D.C. National Guard's ability to deploy without his personal permission. This move was a departure from the norm. Major General William J. Walker, who had been in command of the D.C. National Guard since March 2018, had previously possessed the authority to respond to civil disturbances in the District without seeking explicit approval. Now, the rules were changing, and it was unclear how this would impact the events to come.

On January 4, D.C. Mayor Bowser made a significant announcement. She declared that the Metropolitan Police Department of the District of Columbia (MPD) would lead law enforcement efforts in the district and would coordinate with other agencies, including the Capitol Police, the U.S. Park Police, and the Secret Service. The allocation of responsibilities highlighted the complex web of agencies involved in securing the city during this pivotal time.

During a meeting with a representative of the Capitol Police, Mayor Bowser asked a crucial question: "Where does your perimeter start?" The response, or rather the lack of one, raised concerns. The individual left the room, refusing to engage in further discussion. In hindsight, this moment should have been a red flag, signaling potential issues with the preparations for January 6.

Then came January 6, a day that would go down in infamy. The Capitol Police, under orders from their leadership, deployed without "less lethal" arms such as sting grenades. Riot shields, critical for crowd control, were improperly stored, leading to them shattering upon impact. These unexpected developments hinted at a lack of readiness, a deficiency that would become painfully evident as events unfolded.

Trump supporters gather in D.C.

As the sun dipped below the horizon on the evening of January 5, 2023, the tension in and around the National Mall in Washington, D.C. was palpable. It was a night etched in history, a night that would forever be associated with the events that unfolded the following day.

In the hours leading up to that fateful day, the National Mall was a hive of activity. Freedom Plaza, the North Inner Gravel Walkway between 13th and 14th Streets, Area 9 across from the Russell Senate Office Building, and the vicinity of the United States Supreme Court were all hotspots of political fervor and unrest.

In the pre-dawn hours of January 6, at least ten individuals found themselves in handcuffs, several of them on weapons charges. The arrests on the night of January 5 had cast a shadow of anticipation over the nation's capital.

Among those present on January 5 was Ray Epps, a figure with a history tied to the Arizona Oath Keepers. Epps, a man caught on camera during two street gatherings on January 5, captured the attention of many. In one video, he passionately urged the crowds to enter the Capitol the next day, all while emphasizing that this should be done "peacefully."

However, what struck many as remarkable was that Epps was filmed on January 6 doing just that –

urging people to "go to the Capitol." It raised questions about his true intentions and his role in the events that would soon spiral into chaos. Epps, in a text message to his nephew, had even claimed to be "orchestrating" the flow of individuals into the Capitol building, leaving the nation in suspense about the extent of his involvement.

Yet, in the aftermath, Epps would assert that he had been merely boasting about "directing" people towards the Capitol, leaving a trail of confusion that investigators would struggle to untangle.

On the preceding day, from 1:00 to 5:00 pm, the Freedom Plaza became the epicenter of a series of rallies organized in support of then-former President Donald Trump. The atmosphere was charged with fervor, as passionate supporters gathered to hear influential voices in the pro-Trump movement.

Among the notable speakers were figures who had received presidential pardons just weeks prior. One of them was retired U.S. Army General Michael Flynn, who had pleaded guilty to "willfully and knowingly" making false statements to the FBI about communications with the Russian ambassador. Despite his legal troubles, Flynn remained a prominent proponent of the QAnon conspiracy theory. His presence at the D.C. events on January 5 was a testament to his unwavering support for the former president.

Interestingly, Flynn's brother, U.S. Army General Charles Flynn, played a pivotal role in the unfolding events. On the morning of January 6, as the chaos unfolded at the Capitol, Charles Flynn was involved in a conference call. In a move that would later spark controversy, he denied permission to deploy the National Guard to quell the escalating situation, leaving many to question the response of law enforcement to the breach of the Capitol.

Another key speaker at the January 5 rallies was Roger Stone, a figure with a history of legal troubles. Stone had been found guilty at trial of witness tampering, making false statements to Congress, and obstruction. His involvement with groups like the Proud Boys and the Oath Keepers added an extra layer of intrigue to the events.

What added to the intrigue was Stone's decision to employ Oath Keepers as security on January 5, a decision that would have far-reaching consequences. One of Stone's Oath Keeper associates would later be convicted of seditious conspiracy for their role in plotting and executing the attack on the Capitol on January 6, adding yet another layer of complexity to the events of that day.

As the sun set on January 5, and the nation held its breath, little did anyone know that the events of the following day would reshape the course of American history. The echoes of that night and the voices that rang out on Freedom Plaza would continue to reverberate for years to come, leaving an indelible mark on the nation's consciousness.

High-Stakes Gathering at Trump International Hotel

The night of January 5 was not just marked by rallies and speeches; it was a night of secret meetings and ominous developments that would cast a long shadow over the events of January 6.

Behind the scenes, Trump's closest allies were huddled together at the luxurious Trump International Hotel in Washington, D.C. The gathering was attended by an eclectic mix of individuals, including Michael Flynn, Corey Lewandowski, and Alabama Senator Tommy Tuberville, as well as Trump's own sons, Donald Jr. and Eric. While Tuberville has since claimed he did not attend this meeting, photographs placed him squarely in the hotel's lobby that evening.

According to Charles Herbster, who was present at the gathering, the attendees included Tuberville, Adam Piper, and Peter Navarro. In a detailed account, Daniel Beck described the event as follows: "Fifteen of us spent the evening with Donald Trump Jr., Kimberly Guilfoyle, Tommy Tuberville, Mike Lindell, Peter Navarro, and Rudy Giuliani." Herbster even claimed to be standing "in the private residence of the President at Trump International" with this group of prominent figures and added David Bossie to the list of attendees.

These closed-door discussions and the mix of individuals present raised many questions about their intentions and what strategies were being devised.

Pence's Dilemma and Perceived Threats

While these secretive meetings were taking place, Vice President Mike Pence faced a significant dilemma. He had become a central figure in the unfolding events. On January 5, after Pence publicly stated that he would not participate in the plot to overturn the election results with "fake electors," Trump openly warned that he might have to publicly criticize his Vice President.

This public rift sent shockwaves through the political landscape, but it also had more immediate consequences. Worried for Pence's safety, his chief of staff took the extraordinary step of alerting Pence's Secret Service detail to a perceived threat. The tension and uncertainty surrounding Pence's role would continue to escalate as the events of January 6 loomed.

Bombs Placed: A Sinister Prelude

As the clock ticked toward midnight on January 5, another sinister development unfolded in the shadows. At 7:40 p.m. on that ominous evening, an individual wearing a gray hooded sweatshirt, a mask, and Nike Air Max Speed Turf sneakers was captured on camera. They were seen carrying a bag through a residential neighborhood on South Capitol Street.

Later that evening, at 7:52 p.m., the same individual was recorded sitting on a bench outside the Democratic National Committee (DNC) headquarters. Chillingly, the following day, a pipe bomb was discovered under a bush near that very bench. In the surveillance footage, the suspect could be seen zipping up a bag, then standing and walking away. The danger was growing closer.

But that was not the end of it. At 8:14 p.m. that same night, the individual was filmed in an alley near the Republican National Committee (RNC) headquarters. It was in this alley that a second pipe bomb would be discovered the following day. Both bombs had been placed within a few blocks of the Capitol, in a calculated act of terror.

As of September 2023, nearly two years after these disturbing events, no suspects had been named in connection with the planting of these bombs, despite the reward for information having been upped to $500,000. The mystery surrounding this sinister prelude to January 6 would persist, leaving many to wonder about the identities and motivations of those responsible.

"Save America" Rally and the Unfolding Drama

The dawn of January 6 heralded the much-anticipated "Save America" rally, a gathering that would forever be etched into the annals of American history. Positioned in the heart of the National Mall, on the Ellipse just south of the White House, this rally held the promise of being a defining moment.

Women for America First had secured a permit for their first amendment rally, aptly titled the "March for Trump." The day's events were scheduled to kick off at 9:00 a.m., with speeches slated to run until 3:30 p.m., followed by an additional hour for the conclusion of the rally and the peaceful dispersal of participants.

The Ellipse quickly filled with fervent Trump supporters, eager to hear from their leader and other prominent figures. Among the speakers were former President Donald Trump himself, his personal lawyer Rudy Giuliani, and legal scholar John C. Eastman from Chapman University School of Law. Eastman's role in the event would later come under scrutiny, as his memorandums were described as an instruction manual for a coup d'état.

In a twist that added intrigue to the rally, a member of the Oath Keepers claimed in a court filing in February that she had served as "security" at the event and had been granted a "VIP pass to the rally where she met with Secret Service agents." However, this assertion raised eyebrows, and the U.S. Secret Service categorically denied that any private citizens had coordinated with them to provide security on January 6. Later, on February 22, the Oath Keeper member changed her story, stating that she had only interacted with the Secret Service during the routine security check before the rally.

The stage was set for a day of passionate speeches and incendiary rhetoric. Mo Brooks, a Republican Congressman from Alabama, took the podium around 9 a.m. His words reverberated through the crowd as he declared, "Today is the day American patriots start taking down names and kicking ass." He implored the attendees with a resounding question: "Are you willing to do what it takes to fight for America?" The response from the crowd was thunderous.

Representative Madison Cawthorn from North Carolina added fuel to the fiery atmosphere, proclaiming, "This crowd has some fight." Amy Kremer, addressing the audience, left no room for ambiguity, declaring, "it is up to you and I to save this Republic" and urged them to "keep up the fight."

The Trump family was also in attendance, with Donald Trump Jr. and Eric Trump, along with Eric's wife Lara Trump, taking the stage. They did not mince words, naming and verbally attacking Republican congressmen and senators who had not supported efforts to challenge the Electoral College vote. Promising future political battles, Donald Jr. delivered a pointed message, saying, "If you're gonna be the zero and not the hero, we're coming for you."

But perhaps the most dramatic moment came when Rudy Giuliani, President Trump's personal attorney, took the microphone. Giuliani repeated conspiracy theories about the integrity of the election, asserting that voting machines used were "crooked." In a chilling moment, at 10:50 a.m., he called for "trial by combat," an utterance that sent shockwaves through the crowd.

John C. Eastman, the legal scholar, added his own layer of intrigue by suggesting that ballot machines contained "secret folders" that had manipulated voting results. The crowd was electrified by these claims, and tensions soared.

At 10:58 a.m., a contingent of Proud Boys, a far-right group, abruptly left the rally and marched determinedly toward the Capitol Building. The nation watched in suspense as events began to take a perilous turn.

As if the tension surrounding the "Save America" rally wasn't enough, parallel protests added to the combustible mix. The "Wild Protest," organized by Stop The Steal, unfolded in Area 8, across from the Russell Senate Office Building. Simultaneously, the "Freedom Rally," organized by Virginia Freedom Keepers, Latinos for Trump, and the United Medical Freedom Super PAC, took place at 300 First Street NE, another location near the Russell Senate Office Building.

The streets of Washington, D.C. were a tapestry of competing voices, passions, and grievances. The nation held its breath, unaware that the day would take a dramatic and dangerous turn, altering the course of American history in ways that no one could have foreseen.

Trump's knowledge of weapons in the crowd

In the heart of the storm that was brewing on January 5, former President Donald Trump played a pivotal role, one that would be scrutinized for years to come. Trump, well aware of the passionate crowd gathered around him, had an inkling that some of his supporters were armed, adding an extra layer of tension to the already charged atmosphere.

During the rally, Trump's awareness of the crowd's armament became evident. He demanded that those armed be allowed entry into the rally grounds. His instructions, at times, seemed to teeter on the edge of recklessness as he urged the crowd to march on the hallowed grounds of the United States Capitol.

What followed was a sequence of events that would forever be etched in the annals of American history. In a December 21, 2021, statement, Trump made a false claim, referring to the attack as a "completely unarmed protest." This assertion, however, was far from the truth.

The Department of Justice, in an official statement released in January 2022, revealed the stark reality. Over 75 individuals had been charged in connection with the attack, facing allegations of entering a restricted area with "a dangerous or deadly weapon." Among these individuals were those armed with guns, stun guns, knives, batons, baseball bats, axes, and even chemical sprays.

The weapons in the crowd painted a chilling picture of the events that would soon transpire.

Cassidy Hutchinson, whose role in these events would later become a focal point, provided crucial testimony. According to her account, a Secret Service official had issued a stark warning to Trump, informing him that protestors within the crowd were carrying weapons. The gravity of the situation was clear.

However, Trump's response was nothing short of controversial. In the face of this warning, he brazenly demanded the removal of the magnetometers, devices designed to detect metallic weapons. His reasoning? He insisted that armed supporters should be allowed entry into the rally grounds.

In Hutchinson's recollection, Trump's words were haunting: ***"I don't f*cking care that they have weapons, they're not here to hurt me. They're not here to hurt me. Take the f*cking mags away. Let my people in. They can march to the Capitol from here, let the people in and take the mags away."***

These words, spoken in the charged atmosphere of that day, would reverberate through history, raising questions about responsibility, intent, and the consequences of words spoken by those in positions of power.

Trump's Incendiary Speech

At precisely 11:58 AM, on that chilling January 6 morning, the eyes of the nation were fixed on President Trump as he stepped behind a formidable bulletproof shield. The words that followed would reverberate across the country and the world.

In his speech, President Trump declared with unyielding conviction that he would "never concede" the election. He lashed out at the media, criticizing them for their role in what he perceived as an unjust electoral outcome. Most notably, he called upon Vice President Pence to do the unthinkable – overturn the election results, something that was unequivocally outside Pence's constitutional power.

As the President spoke, his words were laden with falsehoods and misrepresentations, inciting an already fervent crowd. He did not explicitly call for violence or the invasion of the Capitol, but the imagery he employed was undeniably violent. Trump suggested that his supporters held the power to prevent Joe Biden from taking office, fueling the flames of discontent and rebellion.

Simultaneously, Vice President Pence released a letter to Congress in which he firmly stated that he could not challenge Biden's victory. The stage was set for a dramatic showdown between the President and his Vice President, and the nation held its breath in anticipation.

The March to the Capitol

While the initial plan for the rally called for attendees to remain at the Ellipse until the counting of electoral slates was complete, President Trump had other plans. He repeatedly urged the crowd to march to the Capitol, a directive that would have far-reaching consequences.

Trump implored his supporters to "walk down to the Capitol" and to "cheer on our brave senators and congressmen and women." He hinted that their support might wane for some of these officials, setting the stage for a tumultuous day on Capitol Hill.

Despite his earlier promise to join them, President Trump did not ultimately accompany the crowd to the Capitol. As the counting of Biden's electoral votes loomed, he ominously declared, "We can't let that happen," casting doubts on the legitimacy of Biden's presidency.

In a moment that would go down in infamy, Trump asserted, "most people would stand there at 9:00 in the evening and say, 'I want to thank you very much,' and they go off to some other life, but I said, 'Something's wrong here. Something's really wrong. [It] can't have happened.' And we fight. We fight like Hell, and if you don't fight like Hell, you're not going to have a country anymore."

He rallied his supporters with a call to action, stating that they were "going to the Capitol," with the aim of instilling pride and boldness in the hearts of Republicans who sought to "take back our country."

Trump emphasized that "you'll never take back our country with weakness," insisting that they must exhibit strength. He called upon Congress to count only the electors who had been "lawfully slated," hinting at a contested election process that had long divided the nation.

In a striking denunciation, Trump singled out Representative Liz Cheney (R-WY), declaring, "We've got to get rid of the weak Congresspeople, the ones that aren't any good, the Liz Cheneys of the world." He urged his supporters to "fight much harder" against those he deemed "bad people."

The President's words carried a sense of urgency as he told the crowd that they were "not going to take it any longer." He framed the moment as a last stand, warning that accepting Biden's victory had placed Pence and other Republican officials in grave danger.

Despite his earlier assurance that he would march with them to the Capitol, Trump was ultimately prevented from doing so by his security detail, leaving the crowd to forge ahead without him.

During Trump's impassioned speech, his supporters chanted phrases that would foreshadow the tumultuous events to come. The crowd roared with chants of "Take the Capitol," "Taking the Capitol right now," "Invade the Capitol," "Storm the Capitol," and "Fight for Trump."

These chants, echoing through the air, set the stage for what would become one of the darkest days in American history. Before President Trump had even finished speaking at 1:12 PM, the Proud Boys had already initiated their assault on the Capitol, breaching its outer perimeter. The nation watched in disbelief as the events of that day spiraled out of control, with the very foundations of democracy shaken to their core.

As the clock ticked, the fate of the nation hung in the balance, and the echoes of President Trump's words continued to reverberate across the Capitol, carrying with them a sense of impending crisis that would unfold in ways that no one could have foreseen.

Attack on Capitol

At 10:30 AM, the Washington Monument served as a rallying point for over a hundred Proud Boys, a far-right extremist group, led by figures like Ethan Nordean and Joe Biggs. With a sense of purpose, they set off on a march towards the heart of American democracy, the U.S. Capitol. Little did anyone know the gravity of what was about to transpire.

By 11:52 AM, the group had reached their destination: the hallowed grounds of the Capitol. They didn't rush headlong into chaos; instead, they took a deliberate approach. They began by circling the building, their eyes scanning for any weaknesses in the defenses that guarded the heart of American governance.

As the Proud Boys made their way, a chilling revelation emerged, captured by a documentary filmmaker who was present at the scene. Among the Proud Boys, there was a moment when the veneer of mere protest seemed to fade away. One of them, known by the nickname "Milkshake," was caught on a livestream discussing a plan to storm the Capitol. In hushed tones, Rufio, one of the leaders of the Proud Boys, cautioned, "You could keep that quiet, please, Milkshake." The die had been cast, and a sinister plan was in motion.

Around 12:30 PM, east of the Capitol, a crowd began to swell in numbers. Among them was Senator Josh Hawley from Missouri, a prominent figure in the group of lawmakers who had pledged to challenge the Electoral College vote. He raised a clenched fist in solidarity with the protesters as he made his way to the joint session of Congress that was set to convene in the early afternoon. The stage was set for a day of reckoning.

At 12:52 PM, a group of Oath Keepers, identifiable by their black hoodies adorned with prominent logos, left the rally at the Ellipse. Their attire would soon undergo a transformation. As they made their way to the Capitol, they changed into Army Combat Uniforms and donned helmets, preparing for something far more sinister.

Shortly before 12:53 PM, the Proud Boys, numbering between 200 and 300 strong, were led by Nordean and Biggs to a barricade on the west side of the Capitol grounds, near the Peace Monument. The tension in the air was palpable. Joe

Biggs took to a megaphone, rallying the crowd with chants that reverberated through the hallowed halls of democracy.

The moment was charged with a sense of impending chaos, as if a storm was brewing just beyond the horizon. The Proud Boys, joined by other like-minded individuals, were now positioned at the gates of the Capitol, their intentions veiled but ominous.

Samsel, a figure later thrust into the spotlight, was the first to breach the restricted Capitol grounds. In a video that would later be scrutinized by investigators, Samsel's actions were captured as he crossed a significant threshold. This moment was a turning point, a flashpoint in the events that would soon unravel.

The Proud Boys, at the forefront of the crowd, reached the west perimeter of the Capitol grounds. They found themselves facing a line of police officers guarding a temporary fence. The scene was tense, but the police presence was far from overwhelming, creating a vulnerable situation that would be exploited by the Proud Boys.

As the crowd grew around them, the Proud Boys displayed a tactical prowess that belied their reputation as mere protesters. They meticulously coordinated their attacks, orchestrating the first moments of violence that would escalate into multiple breaches of the Capitol. Their strategy was cunning; they aimed to give the impression that they were ordinary protesters leading the charge, masking their more sinister intentions.

A "tipping point" occurred when Ryan Samsel approached Joe Biggs, the Proud Boys' leader. Their conversation, as recounted later by Samsel to the FBI, revealed the manipulation and intimidation tactics used by Biggs. Samsel claimed that Biggs had encouraged him to push at the barricades, and when he hesitated, the Proud Boys' leader had allegedly brandished a gun, questioning Samsel's manhood and repeating his demand to move to the front and confront the police. This encounter encapsulated the volatile mix of bravado and aggression that defined the events of that day.

Proud Boy Dominic Pezzola, an eyewitness to this exchange, recalled seeing Biggs flash a handgun and goading Samsel to "defend his manhood" by attacking the police line. However, Pezzola later attempted to retract his statement, reflecting the complexity and fear that permeated the atmosphere that day.

Caroline Edwards, a Capitol police officer, vividly described the ensuing chaos. She recounted how Biggs had encouraged Samsel to approach the bike rack barricade where she was posted. Samsel's actions led to the bike rack being pushed over, causing her to strike her head and lose consciousness. In those moments before blacking out, Edwards witnessed what she could only describe as "a war scene." Police officers were bleeding, some were vomiting, and the scene was nothing short of carnage.

Video footage captured the harrowing ordeal as Officer Edwards was pushed behind a bicycle rack while Proud Boys pushed barricades toward her, knocking her off her feet and causing her to collide with the concrete steps. The brutality and violence displayed were unlike anything she had ever witnessed in her career.

The Proud Boys, emboldened by their initial success, led the charge toward the Capitol's next police line. Their tactics were consistent: identifying access points to the building, riling up other protesters, and sometimes directly engaging in acts of violence. When met with resistance, the group's leaders, including Joe Biggs, quickly recalibrated their approach. Teams of Proud Boys shifted their focus to new entry points into the Capitol, maintaining a relentless drive to breach its hallowed halls.

As the events unfolded, it became clear that the Proud Boys were not merely passive participants in the chaos that engulfed the Capitol. They were a driving force, with a calculated strategy that aimed to disrupt the democratic process and challenge the very foundations of American governance. The scenes that played out that day were a stark reminder of the fragility of democracy and the enduring consequences of those pivotal moments in history.

The crowd, brimming with intensity and anger, surged forward, sweeping past barriers and officers. Some members of the mob resorted to extreme measures, spraying officers with noxious chemical agents or viciously striking them with lead pipes. The atmosphere grew increasingly chaotic as the rioters breached the outer defenses.

Amid the mayhem, many rioters made their way up the external stairways, while others opted for makeshift ropes and ladders, reminiscent of a siege from a bygone era. The police desperately tried to block access to a tunnel at the lower west terrace, where rioters waged a grueling three-hour battle to gain entry. In their determination, several rioters scaled the west wall, defying all obstacles in their path.

Inside the Capitol, Representative Zoe Lofgren (D-CA) was acutely aware that the rioters had reached the Capitol steps. Panic gripped her as she tried to reach Capitol Police Chief Steven Sund by phone, but to no avail. House Sergeant-at-Arms Paul D. Irving delivered a chilling message to Lofgren: the doors to the Capitol were locked, and "nobody can get in." It was a moment that underscored the gravity of the situation.

Behind the scenes, telephone logs released by the United States Capitol Police (USCP) revealed a frantic coordination effort led by Chief Sund. His first call was to the D.C. Metropolitan Police, who managed to arrive within a mere 15 minutes of the call. However, Sund's next move was critical. He urgently contacted Irving and Senate Sergeant-at-Arms Michael Stenger at 12:58, requesting an emergency declaration necessary to call in the National Guard. Their response was one of hesitation, as they assured Sund that they would "run it up the chain." But formal approval for the

Guard's deployment was withheld for over an agonizing hour.

Trump's Role in the Chaos

Meanwhile, just as the chaos was escalating, former President Donald Trump, whose rhetoric had fueled the fervor of his supporters, made a fateful decision. At 1:00 p.m., following a fiery speech, Trump ordered his Secret Service detail to drive him to the Capitol. The response he received was a refusal. In a shocking turn of events, it's reported that Trump assaulted his Secret Service driver, attempting to seize control and lunging for the man's throat. This moment of chaos at the highest level of government only added to the turmoil unfolding on Capitol Hill.

As the minutes ticked away, a group of Proud Boys, including prominent figure Joe Biggs, emerged as a key force driving the breach of the Capitol Building. Whether by luck, real-time trial and error, or advance knowledge, these attackers managed to bypass 15 reinforced windows and honed in on the vulnerable recessed area near the Senate. Here, two unreinforced windows and two doors with unreinforced glass were the only barriers standing between them and their objective.

Around 1:12 p.m., reinforcements from the Metropolitan Police Department (MPD), equipped with crowd control gear, arrived on the lower west terrace, attempting to stem the tide of chaos. However, the Proud Boys' strategy was evident.

From 1:25 to 1:28, they executed tactical maneuvers, marching in stack formations away from the newly-reinforced police line.

After observing for about fifteen minutes, the Proud Boys re-entered the fray, targeting two new access points that were poorly defended. Ronald Loehrke and other Proud Boys led a contingent to the east side of the Capitol, where they again employed distraction and teamwork to remove barricades. Their actions prompted the previously peaceful crowd on the east side to overrun barriers along the entire police line.

On the west side, Joe Biggs led a team of Proud Boys targeting the stairs covered by temporary scaffolding. Within two minutes of their arrival, a team of over a dozen Proud Boys approached the entrance to the scaffolding and engaged in a ferocious clash with the police. One of the leaders, known as Daniel "Milkshake" Scott, led the charge, and a harrowing 20-minute battle for control of the scaffolding ensued.

As the tumultuous afternoon unfolded, the on-scene MPD incident commander made a sobering declaration. At 1:50 p.m., they officially declared the situation a riot. It was a moment that underscored the severity of the crisis and the dire need for intervention.

By 1:58 p.m., Capitol Police officers took a fateful step, removing a barricade on the northeast side of the Capitol. This act allowed hundreds of protestors to stream onto the Capitol grounds, a turning point that would further escalate the chaos that had consumed the nation's capital.

Attackers on west terrace breach Senate Wing hallway

The clock neared 2:00 p.m., and the tension outside the Capitol reached its peak. What had been a tumultuous day was about to take a dramatic and dangerous turn. The attackers, fueled by a sense of purpose, reached the doors and windows of the Capitol, determined to breach its defenses.

The Los Angeles Times would later ponder whether it was sheer luck, real-time trial and error, or advanced knowledge that guided the initial attackers. They embarked on a perilous journey, running past 15 reinforced windows, seemingly making a beeline for a specific target – the upper west terrace. This terrace held a secret vulnerability, where two unreinforced windows and two doors with unreinforced glass were the only barriers standing between the attackers and their goal.

At precisely 2:11 p.m., a man named Dominic Pezzola, a leader of the Proud Boys, seized a stolen police riot shield and wielded it like a battering ram. With a forceful blow, he shattered one of those unreinforced windows on the west side of the Capitol. It was a chilling moment as the Capitol's defenses were officially breached at 2:13 p.m.

While most of the Capitol's windows had been fortified, the attackers zeroed in on those that remained as single-pane glass. These windows, they knew, could be shattered with relative ease. The breach had begun, and the fate of the Capitol hung in the balance.

Joe Biggs and other leaders of the Proud Boys swiftly entered the Capitol by 2:14 p.m. Their presence marked a turning point in the unfolding events. As they surged into the heart of American democracy, the world watched in disbelief.

Amidst the chaos, a news crew from British broadcaster ITV made a daring decision – they followed the rioters into the Capitol, becoming the only broadcast team to do so. Their cameras captured the mayhem as it unfolded within the hallowed halls of the Capitol building, offering viewers a raw and unfiltered glimpse into the events that would go down in history.

As the Capitol was being breached, Vice President Mike Pence found himself in a perilous situation. At 2:13 p.m., his lead Secret Service agent, Tim Giebels, took swift action to remove him from the Senate chamber. Pence was ushered into a nearby office, a mere 100 feet from the landing. In that moment, Pence's wife, Karen Pence, their daughter Charlotte Pence Bond, and his brother, Greg Pence, who was a member of the House (R-IN), were also inside the Capitol.

The vice president and his family were just moments away from potentially being seen by the rioters. It was a narrow escape, a twist of fate that could have had catastrophic consequences. The halls of the Capitol, where democracy should have been flourishing, had been plunged into chaos and uncertainty.

Amidst the turmoil, one figure emerged as a hero in the eyes of many. Capitol Police officer Eugene Goodman, unaccompanied by other officers, found himself confronting the angry mob. His actions in those critical minutes would earn him praise and recognition for heroism.

Goodman's quick thinking and fearless bravery played a crucial role in diverting the rioters away from the Senate chamber. As the crowd approached a landing that provided a clear path to the chamber, Goodman made a split-second decision. He pushed the lead attacker, Doug Jensen, and then strategically retreated in the opposite direction, leading the mob away from the chamber.

In essence, Goodman tricked them, willingly becoming the prey to their wolf pack. His actions saved lives, including those of the rioters themselves, as it led them away from the chambers where armed officers were ready to defend. It was a moment of incredible courage and presence of mind.

Those who were present at the time, including Democratic and Republican legislators and members of the press, showered Goodman with praise for his quick thinking and fearless actions. Republican Senator Ben Sasse would later credit

Goodman with "single-handedly preventing untold bloodshed."

Video footage captured by HuffPost reporter Igor Bobic immortalized Goodman's heroism. The video went viral on the internet, amassing over 10 million views, a testament to the impact of his actions on the nation's collective consciousness. A second video of Goodman's confrontation with the crowd was published by ProPublica, further highlighting his incredible bravery.

Goodman's heroism didn't go unnoticed. He was awarded the Congressional Gold Medal and the Presidential Citizens Medal, accolades that reflected the magnitude of his actions on that fateful day. His story would forever be etched into the annals of American history as a symbol of courage in the face of chaos and danger.

Evacuation of leadership amid Capitol lockdown

As the clock struck 2:15 on that fateful afternoon of January 6, the hallowed halls of the United States Capitol bore witness to a scene of unprecedented chaos and turmoil. The Senate, in the midst of one of its most crucial sessions, was abruptly gaveled into recess. Simultaneously, the chamber's imposing doors were secured, serving as a last line of defense against the surging tide of rioters.

A mere minute later, the ominous banging of fists against these very doors echoed through the gallery just outside the Senate chamber. The rioters, consumed by a fervor that knew no bounds, were making their presence known with an unrelenting determination.

Meanwhile, in the ornate chamber of the House of Representatives, Speaker Nancy Pelosi found herself in a precarious situation. With the tumultuous events unfolding around her, she was swiftly escorted out of the chamber, leaving behind an atmosphere of uncertainty and apprehension. The House, like its counterpart across the rotunda, was also gaveled into a sudden recess, casting a shadow over the hallowed halls of democracy.

Inside the Senate chamber, as the ominous banging continued outside, a solitary figure stood resolute. A police officer, armed with a semi-automatic weapon, positioned themselves between the formidable figures of then-Senate Majority Leader Mitch McConnell and then-Senate Minority Leader Chuck Schumer, both stalwarts of their respective parties. The symbolism was unmistakable – a line drawn in the sand, a last-ditch effort to safeguard the heart of American democracy.

In the midst of this turmoil, Senator Mitt Romney of Utah, his frustration evident, raised his hands in exasperation. In a moment of raw candor, he directed his ire at several fellow Republicans who were vehemently challenging the electoral votes that would affirm Joe Biden as the President-elect. His words, laden with a sense of urgency, rang out across the chamber: "This is what you've gotten, guys."

Amidst this tumult, a group of dedicated individuals worked tirelessly to preserve the sanctity of the Electoral College votes and the documentation that accompanied them. Members of Senate parliamentarian Elizabeth MacDonough's staff, with determination etched on their faces, carried the boxes containing these critical documents out of the chamber. Their destination: hidden safe rooms within the Capitol building, where the cherished symbols of democracy would find refuge amidst the storm.

Outside the chambers, the nation and the world watched in disbelief as the events unfolded. At 2:24 pm, then-President Donald Trump took to Twitter to air his grievances. In a message filled with thinly veiled frustration, he declared that Vice President Mike Pence "didn't have the courage to do what should have been done." The tweet sent shockwaves through the nation and added fuel to the already raging fire.

On the far-right reaches of social media, Trump's most ardent followers amplified the sentiment. Calls for Pence to be tracked down reverberated through the digital landscape, and the frenzied mob within the Capitol began chanting a sinister refrain: "Where is Pence?" and "Find Mike Pence!" The air was thick with tension and menace.

Outside the Capitol's formidable walls, the chants grew even darker. The mob, inflamed by a dangerous fervor, cried out, "Hang Mike Pence!" It was a chilling refrain, one that would haunt the collective conscience of the nation for years to come. Some among the raucous crowd even declared their sinister intentions, vowing to find Pence and execute him as a "traitor," with grim plans to hang him from a tree just outside the very building where democracy had once stood so resolutely.

In the midst of this chaos, those tasked with protecting Vice President Pence were gripped by fear. Members of the Vice President's Secret Service detail found themselves in a nightmarish scenario. They screamed in terror, their voices reflecting the gravity of the situation. They uttered chilling words like "say goodbye to the family," as the specter of violence loomed over them.

As the nation grappled with the unthinkable, shocking revelations emerged from within the White House itself. White House chief of staff Mark Meadows reportedly conveyed a disturbing message. President Trump, in his anger at Pence's evacuation to safety, allegedly made a chilling suggestion – a suggestion that would send shockwaves through the corridors of power. The president hinted that Pence should be hanged, a statement that underscored the gravity of the situation and the depths to which the nation had descended.

As the clock struck 2:26 on that chilling January afternoon, the unthinkable was already in motion. Vice President Mike Pence and his family had been evacuated from their concealed location near the

Senate, moving hurriedly toward a more secure refuge. Pence was a pivotal figure in the unfolding crisis, and his actions in the coming hours would be scrutinized by the nation.

The Secret Service detail assigned to protect Pence urged him to leave the vicinity of the Capitol, their primary concern being his safety. However, Pence, displaying a rare moment of resolve, declined to enter the waiting vehicle. With unwavering trust in his lead agent, Tim Giebels, he uttered the words, "I trust you, Tim, but you're not driving the car."

In the wake of this evacuation, chaos engulfed the entire Capitol complex. All buildings were placed on lockdown, sealing them off from the outside world. Capitol staff found themselves in a dire situation, with no entry or exit permitted. A stark message reverberated through the hallways and offices: "Shelter in place."

As the mob descended upon the Capitol, the elected representatives, their aides, and support staff were thrust into a nightmare scenario. They sought refuge in offices, closets, and any available hiding spot, their hearts pounding with anxiety and fear.

In a room adjacent to a hallway, aides to Senate Majority Leader Mitch McConnell huddled together, their senses heightened by the noise just beyond their barricaded door. Outside, a rioter could be heard, their voice raised in an unsettling prayer, a desperate plea for "the evil of Congress [to] be brought to an end." The walls of the Capitol, once a symbol of democracy, now bore witness to a surreal descent into lawlessness.

The invaders showed no restraint, even targeting the office of the Senate Parliamentarian, ransacking it with impunity. The hallowed halls of democracy were being desecrated by those who believed they were fulfilling a misguided mission.

While this nightmare unfolded, a political drama of unimaginable proportions played out in the Senate chamber itself. With senators still in their seats, President Donald Trump reached out to Senator Tommy Tuberville (R-AL) via phone. Trump implored Tuberville to take additional steps to block the counting of Joe Biden's electoral votes.

However, before any decisive action could be taken, the Senate chamber was evacuated at precisely 2:30, further fracturing the already tumultuous proceedings. The invaders wasted no time seizing the opportunity, briefly taking control of the chamber. Among them, some individuals carried plastic handcuffs, while others defiantly raised their fists on the Senate dais, a podium vacated by Vice President Pence just minutes earlier.

The chaos inside the Capitol was met with swift responses. Staff and reporters, caught in the midst of the pandemonium, were swiftly ushered into secure elevators. These elevators descended into the bowels of the Capitol, leading to an underground bunker constructed in the aftermath of the attempted attack on the Capitol in 2001.

However, even these precautions were not enough to deter the relentless mob. As evacuees made their way towards safety, their route was suddenly redirected when it became apparent that the bunker itself had been infiltrated by the very individuals they were fleeing from. The unthinkable had become reality.

Sergeant-at-Arms of the Senate, Michael C. Stenger, found himself in the unenviable position of shepherding a group of senators, including the likes of Lindsey Graham (R-SC) and Joe Manchin (D-WV), to a secure location within a Senate office building. The lawmakers, their emotions ranging from shock to fury, had pressing questions for Stenger. Graham's voice rang out, demanding answers, "How does this happen? How does this happen?" Their resolve was clear - they would not be driven from their duty by a rampaging mob.

In the midst of this chaos, the House of Representatives was a battleground in its own right. Representative Dean Phillips (D-MN) could no longer contain his frustration, shouting at his Republican colleagues, "This is because of you!" The partisan fault lines were never more apparent, as the blame game unfolded amidst the turmoil.

The House attempted to resume its debate around 2:25, but the situation deteriorated rapidly. By 2:30, Representative Paul Gosar had finished speaking, and the House was forced into yet another recess. Rioters had breached the House wing, and their presence outside the Speaker's Lobby, just steps from the chamber, was a clear and present danger.

Lawmakers, still within the chamber, were hastily evacuated. Among them, Speaker Nancy Pelosi, House Minority Leader Kevin McCarthy, and a handful of their colleagues were ushered to a secure location. Violence had erupted, and Capitol security urged members of Congress to take cover.

Inside the House chamber, a surreal scene unfolded as lawmakers donned gas masks. Tear gas had been deployed within the building, adding yet another layer of danger and disorientation to an already nightmarish scenario. The air itself was now a hostile force.

Amidst this chaos, ABC News reported the sound of gunfire echoing through the hallowed halls of the Capitol. An armed standoff played out at the front door of the House of Representatives chamber. Federal law enforcement officers, their weapons drawn, pointed them toward the barricaded doors, behind which the mob raged.

Inside a stairwell, a moment of desperation unfolded as an officer discharged a shot at an individual approaching, the echoes of the gunshot serving as a stark reminder of the violence that had erupted.

Even the sanctity of press credentials was not spared. Photographer Erin Schaff, who had bravely ventured into the Capitol Rotunda, suddenly found herself under threat. Rioters seized her press badge, and the situation escalated further when police, unaware of her credentials being stolen, held her at gunpoint. It was only through the intervention of her colleagues that disaster was averted.

The shocking revelation that panic buttons had been tampered with sent shockwaves through the House of Representatives. The chief of staff for Representative Ayanna Pressley (D-MA) made a chilling claim that all the panic buttons in the office had been torn out, leaving them vulnerable and defenseless. The missing buttons, initially raising concerns of sabotage, would later be explained as a "clerical screw-up" by a House Administration Committee email. Yet, the sense of vulnerability lingered.

The invaders, emboldened by their actions, documented their occupation of the Capitol with their cell phone cameras. They brazenly entered the offices of various representatives, vandalizing and desecrating the very symbols of democracy. Speaker Pelosi's office was not spared, as rioters wreaked havoc, leaving an indelible stain on the heart of American governance.

But perhaps the most shocking act of all was the theft of a laptop, a device that contained sensitive and confidential information. As the sun set on that harrowing day, the nation watched in disbelief as the Capitol, a beacon of democracy, became a battleground of chaos and insurrection. The echoes of that dark day would reverberate through history, forever changing the course of the United States.

January 6 Committee testimony

The sixth televised hearing held by the congressional committee investigating the tumultuous events surrounding January 6 was one that had the nation on the edge of its seat. This particular hearing was dedicated entirely to the testimony of Cassidy Hutchinson, a key figure who served as a top aide to former White House Chief of Staff Mark Meadows.

The anticipation leading up to this hearing was electric. Meadows had initially cooperated with the committee, providing a substantial trove of documents and information. However, the tide had shifted, and he abruptly ceased his cooperation, casting a shadow of doubt over what he might be hiding. Matters escalated further when Meadows took the extraordinary step of suing the committee, a move that left many wondering about the secrets he might be protecting. His defiance reached its peak when he was held in criminal contempt of Congress in December 2021, a historic event that reverberated through the halls of power.

The heightened security concerns surrounding Hutchinson's testimony were evident. The committee's announcement of the hearing came with barely a day's notice, underscoring the gravity of the situation. It was a testament to the sensitivity of the information she held and the potential ramifications of her words.

Ms. Hutchinson, well aware of the stakes, took her own measures to ensure her safety before stepping into the public eye. The fact that she felt compelled to secure her own security spoke volumes about the gravity of the revelations she might make. It was a reflection of the immense pressure that came with bearing witness to history.

Inside the hearing room, tension hung thick in the air, palpable to all who watched. The committee, too, had taken measures to enhance its security for this pivotal sixth hearing. The nation waited with bated breath as Cassidy Hutchinson took her place at the witness stand, ready to share her insights into the events that had shaken the very foundations of American democracy.

A Prelude to January 6

It all began on January 2 when Rudy Giuliani, the former mayor of New York City and a staunch ally of then-President Trump, delivered a message that would send shivers down Hutchinson's spine. Giuliani confided in her, revealing a plan that would shape the course of history. Trump and his closest allies were intending to march to the Capitol on January 6.

Hutchinson, grappling with the gravity of this information, knew she had to report it to her boss, Mark Meadows, who served as White House Chief of Staff at the time. However, when she approached him with this ominous revelation, Meadows' reaction was far from reassuring. He remained fixated on his phone, offering only a cryptic response, "things might get real, real bad." It was a chilling acknowledgment of the impending storm that loomed over the nation's capital.

But this was just the tip of the iceberg. Hutchinson's testimony before the committee unveiled a web of intrigue that surrounded the events leading up to January 6.

Hutchinson's testimony provided crucial insight into the planning of the January 6 rally. She revealed that during discussions, both the Proud Boys and Oath Keepers, two prominent extremist groups, were mentioned. What's more intriguing is that these mentions often occurred in the presence of Rudy Giuliani, adding an unsettling dimension to the narrative.

As the committee delved deeper, it became clear that there was a concerted effort to distance the White House from the impending march on the Capitol. White House counsel Pat Cipollone played a pivotal role in this endeavor. Hutchinson recounted a conversation where Cipollone urged caution, telling her, "Please make sure we don't go up to the Capitol, Cass. ... We are going to get charged with every crime imaginable." It was a stark warning of the legal perils that awaited anyone associated with the White House who ventured towards the Capitol on that ominous day.

Perhaps one of the most intriguing aspects of Hutchinson's testimony was her influence over Mark Meadows' decisions on the eve of January 6. She recounted persuading Meadows not to physically attend what was ominously referred to as Giuliani and John Eastman's "war room" at the Willard Hotel on the evening of January 5. This war room was a hub of strategic discussions, and among those present was former National Security Advisor Lt. Gen. Michael Flynn, a figure with his own controversial history.

Meadows, influenced by Hutchinson, decided to forego a physical presence at the war room, opting instead to participate via a phone call. This decision would have profound implications for the events that would soon unfold.

The committee's efforts to unravel the truth extended to General Michael Flynn, who had been subpoenaed. During his interview, Representative Cheney posed a question that struck at the heart of American democracy, "General Flynn, do you believe in the peaceful transition of power in the United States of America?" Flynn's response sent shockwaves through the hearing room as he invoked the Fifth Amendment, refusing to answer the question.

This video clip of Flynn's silence would become a poignant symbol of the turbulence that had engulfed the nation in the wake of the January 6 attack.

The climax of Hutchinson's testimony centered on a revelation that sent shockwaves through the committee. On the very day before the Capitol attack, Trump had issued a directive to Meadows. He was to make contact with two individuals, Lt. Gen. Michael Flynn and Roger Stone, both of whom had deep-rooted ties to extremist groups like the Proud Boys and Oath Keepers.

These connections would later prove to be deeply troubling, as leaders of these extremist groups would face indictments for seditious conspiracy in connection with their alleged roles in the attack on the Capitol.

Hutchinson's Account of January 6

The day began with President Trump preparing to address a massive crowd gathered for the January 6 rally. What many may not know is that Trump had insisted on specific language for his speech, setting the stage for what would follow. Hutchinson's recollections shed light on the legal advice given by Eric Herschmann, a prominent figure advising Trump at the time.

Herschmann had cautioned against the inclusion of certain phrases, deeming them "foolish." Among these were the now-infamous lines, "We're going to March to the Capitol" and "Fight for Trump ... Fight for the movement." These words, Herschmann believed, carried a weight that could potentially incite unrest and violence. The lawyer's counsel extended to discouraging negative references to Vice President Mike Pence, recognizing the potential volatility of the situation.

One chilling aspect of that day was the presence of armed individuals within the crowd gathered to hear Trump's speech. Police radio transmissions would later confirm that some attendees had brought weapons, including AR-15s. What made this revelation all the more unsettling was the fact that Trump, the man at the center of it all, was aware of the armed assembly.

However, rather than expressing concern for his safety, Trump seemed intent on loosening security checks. He specifically demanded the removal of magnetometers, devices designed to detect metal objects, which would have potentially identified weapons among the crowd.

Classidy Hutchinson, who stood among the throngs of Trump's supporters that day, would later testify about a startling statement she overheard from the President himself. Trump, in the midst of a crowd armed to the teeth, reportedly said something to the effect of, "I don't F-ing care that they have weapons. They're not here to hurt me." It was a moment that left many both stunned and bewildered.

As the day progressed, so did the intensity of the mob that had gathered. Calls for Vice President Mike Pence to be hanged reverberated through the air, painting a picture of a nation teetering on the brink of anarchy. Hutchinson, caught in the midst of it all, would bear witness to a pivotal conversation between two influential figures in the Trump administration.

White House Counsel Pat Cipollone and Chief of Staff Mark Meadows engaged in a conversation that would send shockwaves through the corridors of power. Cipollone, recognizing the urgency of the situation and the potential for violence, argued vehemently that they needed to take immediate action to prevent a catastrophe.

However, Meadows, perhaps reflecting Trump's mindset at the time, had a different perspective. He reminded Cipollone of the President's sentiments, asserting that Pence "deserved it." In Trump's eyes, the Vice President was seen as disloyal for not overturning the election results in his favor. Trump reportedly believed that those who had gathered on his behalf "didn't think they're doing anything wrong."

Hutchinson revealed a startling incident that took place on the day that would become etched in history. She testified that, after delivering his speech to a sea of fervent supporters, President Trump expressed a desire to appear in-person at the Capitol. It was a decision that would have far-reaching consequences, and it set the stage for a confrontation that would be remembered for years to come.

Secret Service agent Robert Engel, tasked with ensuring the safety of the President, took a firm stand against Trump's wish to head to the Capitol. In a tense exchange, Engel insisted that it would not be safe for the President to venture into the heart of the unfolding chaos. Instead, he recommended taking Trump to the White House, where he could be secured.

However, the President's determination was unwavering. Hutchinson's testimony recounted the moment when Tony Ornato, another key figure in Trump's security detail, informed her that Trump had become visibly angry and was adamant about going to the Capitol.

What followed was a scene of unprecedented tension. According to Hutchinson, Trump's frustration reached a boiling point. In a shocking moment, she testified that Trump grabbed for the steering wheel of the presidential SUV with one hand while lunging at Engel with the other. It was a desperate, alarming move that left those present stunned.

In Hutchinson's words, Engel, who had been sitting in a chair, appeared "somewhat discombobulated and a little lost" as Ornato relayed the account of these tumultuous events. Notably, Engel did not contradict Hutchinson's version of events, leaving the incident shrouded in mystery and intrigue.

In the days following Hutchinson's explosive testimony, news outlets raced to uncover the truth behind this dramatic confrontation. CNN reported that it had spoken with two Secret Service agents who had heard accounts of the incident from multiple other agents since February 2021. While details differed, one common thread emerged: there had indeed been an angry confrontation. One agent recounted that Trump had "tried to lunge over the seat—for what reason, nobody had any idea." However, it's important to note that no one asserted that Trump physically assaulted Engel.

Politico, in a parallel investigation, revealed that Engel had kept his full account of the incident from his Secret Service colleagues for at least fourteen months. This revelation raised questions about why

Engel had not shared the complete details of the encounter earlier and added to the intrigue surrounding this pivotal moment.

As Hutchinson's testimony echoed through the halls of the committee, it was further bolstered by National Security Council records. These records, which identified Trump by his codename "Mogul," corroborated Hutchinson's claim that security measures were relaxed and that orders were issued to the NSC and Secret Service to "clear a route" for the President.

The significance of this testimony and the supporting evidence could not be overstated. It hinted at a high-stakes clash within the highest echelons of government on a day when the nation watched in shock and disbelief.

Immediate aftermath of January 6

In the aftermath of the tumultuous events of January 6, 2023, Classidy Hutchinson emerged as a pivotal figure in the unfolding saga. Her testimony before the committee investigating the events of that fateful day would shed light on the inner workings of the White House and the individuals who sought to influence the course of history.

During her gripping testimony, Hutchinson revealed a startling revelation that sent shockwaves through the nation. She testified that amidst the chaos of the Capitol riot, she had found herself in a surreal moment, transcribing a proposed statement on behalf of the President of the United States. This statement, as she described it, was a plea for the insurgents to abandon their assault on the Capitol and leave in peace.

The source of this statement was none other than Mark Meadows, the Chief of Staff at the White House during the turbulent final days of the Trump administration. Hutchinson recounted how she diligently wrote down the words from Meadows' dictation, her pen moving as swiftly as her heart pounded.

However, what added a layer of intrigue to this revelation was Hutchinson's mention of White House attorney Eric Herschmann. She testified that as she transcribed Meadows' words, Herschmann "chimed in" with his input. This revelation raised questions about the extent of legal counsel's involvement in crafting a statement that would later be examined under a microscope by investigators and the American public.

The note that Hutchinson had penned, displaying the proposed presidential statement, was a tangible piece of evidence that left no room for doubt. It was presented during the hearing, and Hutchinson confirmed without hesitation that it was indeed in her own handwriting. However, in a twist that only added to the complexity of the situation, Herschmann later claimed through a spokesperson that he had been the one to write the note. The nation was left grappling with the mystery of authorship, a mystery that continued to linger in the halls of power.

But the revelations did not stop there. Hutchinson's testimony unveiled another layer of intrigue that exposed the desperation of some key figures in the aftermath of January 6. She testified that both Mark Meadows and Rudy Giuliani, the former mayor of New York City and staunch Trump supporter, had sought presidential pardons.

This revelation painted a picture of individuals who had been involved in activities that they believed could lead to legal repercussions. The pursuit of presidential pardons spoke volumes about their concerns regarding potential legal consequences for their actions in the lead-up to and during the events of January 6.

As Hutchinson's testimony unfolded, it became evident that the aftermath of January 6 was not merely a story of chaos and violence but also one of political maneuvering and legal strategizing. The quest for presidential pardons underscored the gravity of the situation and raised questions about accountability in the highest echelons of power.

In the closing moments of the hearing, Representative Liz Cheney, a member of the committee, raised concerns that some witnesses may have been subjected to external pressures and messages intended to influence their testimony. It was a startling revelation that added an element of suspense to an already riveting narrative.

Cheney did not name the witness in question but revealed that this individual had informed the committee of receiving multiple messages with a common thread. These messages conveyed the idea that, as long as the witness continued to be a "team player" and protected certain interests, they would remain in good standing within the world of Trump's loyal supporters.

One message, in particular, sent chills down the spines of those present at the hearing. It contained phrases like "he is thinking about you," "he knows you're loyal," and "will do the right thing." These messages were more than just words; they were subtle reminders of the power dynamics at play, the unspoken expectations, and the potential consequences of straying from the path of loyalty.

In a dramatic twist that unfolded two days after the hearing, Politico reported that Classidy Hutchinson was the recipient of the quoted messages. She had received them before her deposition on March 7, and the message that read "he is thinking about you" had come from an intermediary for none other than Mark Meadows.

Cheney, in her closing remarks, made it clear that the committee was taking these allegations of witness tampering seriously. The shadow of external influence cast a pall over the integrity of the investigative process, and Cheney emphasized that they would consider the "next steps" necessary to address this grave issue.

As the nation digested the revelations from Hutchinson's testimony, another layer of complexity emerged. On December 20, 2022, it was reported that Classidy Hutchinson had been advised by Trump administration ethics attorney Stefan

Passantino, who was then her client, to testify that she didn't remember crucial details. What added a twist to this tale was the revelation that Trump's Save America PAC was footing the bill for Passantino's services, a fact that Hutchinson had been unaware of.

Hutchinson's disagreement with Passantino's advice led to her making a pivotal decision. She switched lawyers before her testimony, a move that underscored the ethical dilemmas and potential conflicts of interest that permeated the aftermath of January 6. The role of legal counsel in shaping the narrative and protecting their clients' interests added yet another layer of intrigue to the unfolding drama.

Reaction Hutchinson's Hearing

Hutchinson's testimony wasn't just any ordinary hearing; it was subject to an unprecedented level of national attention. Time Magazine described it as having "garnered a reaction that no other had received to date." As she exited the hearing room, a remarkable sight unfolded. A crowd gathered in the back of the room, and they didn't hold back – they applauded her. It was a spontaneous show of support, a rare occurrence in the solemn halls of Congress.

Fox News host Bret Baier didn't mince words when he commented on her testimony. He said, "Hutchinson's testimony was very compelling from beginning to end." Even conservative commentator

George Conway, known for his sharp critiques, was left astounded. He exclaimed, "This is the most astonishing testimony I have ever seen or heard or read. You could litigate or investigate for a thousand years and never see anything as mind-blowing as this." Such reactions from both sides of the political spectrum showcased the gravity of her words.

The Lawfare blog went further, stating, "Cassidy Hutchinson's Testimony Changed Our Minds about Indicting Donald Trump." These words would reverberate across the nation and contribute to a seismic shift in public perception.

Hutchinson's testimony wasn't just captivating; it was legally significant. Legal analysts and the press immediately recognized the gravity of her words, particularly in the context of possible indictments of Trump and his associates. The Justice Department had launched a criminal investigation into attempts to overturn the 2020 presidential election, and Hutchinson's revelations would send shockwaves through the corridors of power.

Former Trump Attorney General Bill Barr, no stranger to political drama, remarked, "the department is clearly looking into all this, and this hearing definitely gave investigators a lot to chew on." It was a statement laden with implications, hinting at the potential legal consequences that could follow.

In the wake of Hutchinson's testimony, CNN reported a twist in the story. An unnamed "Secret Service official familiar with the matter" came forward to challenge part of her account. This official claimed that Anthony Ornato, the Secret Service agent at the center of her testimony, had denied telling Hutchinson about a physical altercation.

The plot thickened when CNN reported that the Department of Homeland Security (DHS) Office of Legislative Affairs was willing to make involved agents available to the committee for sworn testimony. These agents, it was stated, would be prepared to unequivocally state that the alleged incident did not occur.

However, as time passed, it became clear that the story was far from over. According to Representative Zoe Lofgren, "Some of the officers said that they would be coming and talking under oath ... [But] they have not come in." Instead, key figures like Anthony Ornato, Robert Engel, and the unnamed driver of the president's armored vehicle had all retained legal counsel, suggesting that this story had more layers than met the eye. (It would be months later that the committee would finally interview the driver.)

The Hutchinson testimony had opened a Pandora's box of questions, contradictions, and legal implications. It was a testimony that had the nation on the edge of its seat, waiting for the next twist in a story that had already captivated the collective imagination of the American people.

Tony Ornato: A Key Figure Under Scrutiny

Tony Ornato, who had led Trump's Secret Service detail until December 2019 when he assumed the role of White House deputy chief of staff for operations, found himself at the center of the storm. Ornato's career trajectory was notable in itself. He had taken an unprecedented leave of absence from his civil service Secret Service position to accept the politically charged appointment.

As the nation watched and waited for answers, Politico's report, just two days after Hutchinson's testimony, revealed a growing skepticism among members of the committee regarding Ornato's credibility. This skepticism stemmed from assertions made by Ornato during his January and March depositions.

The question loomed large: Could Ornato be trusted to provide an impartial account of the events, given his close ties to President Trump? Washington Post reporter Carol Leonnig, renowned for her book "Zero Fail: The Rise and Fall of the Secret Service," shed light on this matter. She described Engel and Ornato as individuals who were "very, very close to President Trump," raising concerns about their objectivity.

During an MSNBC interview, Leonnig pulled no punches. She pointed out that some had accused figures like Ornato of being "enablers" and "yes men" for the president. It was suggested that they were individuals who consistently sought to keep the president pleased, sometimes at the expense of impartiality.

Leonnig's revelations didn't stop there. She delved deeper into the complex web of loyalties within Trump's Secret Service detail. Shockingly, she disclosed that there was a significant contingent within the Secret Service who openly expressed their desire for President Biden to fail. Some even took to their personal social media accounts to cheer on the insurrectionists and those who had descended upon the Capitol, referring to them as "patriots."

As the nation grappled with these astonishing claims, the tension in the air was palpable. Two months after Hutchinson's gripping testimony, Ornato, who had since been serving as assistant director of the Secret Service, made a stunning announcement – he was retiring. The timing and circumstances of his departure raised eyebrows, prompting speculation about the underlying reasons.

Conflicting Accounts and Lingering Questions

Ornato's testimony to the committee added yet another layer of complexity to an already convoluted narrative. He professed not to remember informing Hutchinson about any physical altercation between Trump and the limo driver. This revelation left many scratching their heads, wondering about the gaps and inconsistencies in the accounts provided by various witnesses.

The committee, in its final report, noted the difficulty in fully reconciling the accounts offered by these witnesses. While there seemed to be a consensus that Trump had been consumed by anger during the fateful events, the details surrounding any physical altercation remained shrouded in uncertainty.

The nation had witnessed a whirlwind of revelations, and yet, clarity remained elusive. Hutchinson's testimony had ignited a firestorm of scrutiny, turning the spotlight onto figures like Ornato and raising questions about their loyalty and credibility.

Trump's Counterattack on Truth Social

In the immediate aftermath of Hutchinson's testimony, the 45th President of the United States, Donald J. Trump, took to his newly-established platform, Truth Social, to fire back. In classic Trump fashion, he didn't mince words. He disputed the veracity of many of Hutchinson's statements, painting her as a "liar" and a "total phony." It was a direct, no-holds-barred response from the man known for his unfiltered communication style.

Trump's use of Truth Social, a platform he owned and controlled, gave him an unfiltered megaphone to counter Hutchinson's claims. It was a battle of words in the digital arena, a clash between a former president and a witness whose testimony had rocked the nation.

Amidst this digital duel, Fox News anchor Bret Baier weighed in, offering a unique perspective. On June 28, he noted, "Cassidy Hutchinson is under oath on Capitol Hill. The President is on Truth Social ... [Her] testimony in and of itself is really, really powerful." Baier's observation highlighted the gravity of the situation. The nation watched as Hutchinson's words clashed with Trump's denials in real-time, creating a spectacle unlike any other in recent memory.

As the nation grappled with the implications of Hutchinson's testimony, the dark underbelly of conspiracy theories began to surface. On the same day as her hearing, the anonymous and enigmatic figure known as "Q" posted to the imageboard 8kun. In a cryptic message, "Q" claimed that Hutchinson was involved in a plot to disparage Trump, adding yet another layer of intrigue to the ongoing drama. The post sent shockwaves through online communities, as conspiracy theories swirled about Hutchinson's true intentions.

Notable QAnon influencer Jordan Sather chimed in on his Telegram channel, raising doubts about Hutchinson's authenticity. He referred to her as a "plant" and openly questioned whether her testimony was an attempt to undermine the credibility of the hearings. Sather's words reflected the skepticism that had taken hold in certain corners of the internet, where conspiracy theories often flourish.

In the wake of Hutchinson's explosive testimony, the repercussions extended far beyond social media debates and online conspiracies. Conservative author David French, known for his thoughtful analysis, penned an article for The Dispatch titled "The Case for Prosecuting Donald Trump Just Got Much Stronger." In his view, Trump's role in the events of January 6 had become even more legally precarious.

French argued that Trump had demonstrably summoned the mob, knowing it was armed and dangerous, and had exhorted it to "fight like hell." He contended that Hutchinson's sworn testimony had filled a crucial gap in the potential criminal case against Trump. The legal landscape had shifted, and Trump was now closer to facing a credible prosecution than ever before.

The Washington Examiner, a conservative publication widely read by Trump supporters, added its voice to the growing chorus of criticism. In an editorial published the day after Hutchinson's testimony, the paper's board did not hold back. The headline, "Trump proven unfit for power again," conveyed the severity of their stance.

The editorial went on to state, "Cassidy Hutchinson's Tuesday testimony ought to ring the death knell for former President Donald Trump's political career." It was a damning verdict from a publication that had traditionally been sympathetic to Trump's agenda. The paper's board argued that

Trump was a disgrace, and they called for Republicans to consider alternative leadership options for 2024.

In the days following Hutchinson's hearing, the nation was left in a state of political turmoil. Her testimony had ignited a firestorm of debate, legal analysis, and soul-searching within the Republican Party. The battle lines were drawn, and the consequences of that pivotal moment on Capitol Hill would continue to shape the trajectory of American politics for years to come.

As the nation grappled with the fallout, one thing was abundantly clear – Cassidy Hutchinson's words had shaken the foundations of power and brought the question of accountability to the forefront of the American political landscape.

Conclusion

Dear Readers,

As we bring Cassidy Hutchinson's biography to a close, we find ourselves at the intersection of history and human aspiration. It has been a remarkable journey, one filled with twists and turns, hope and disillusionment, and a stark reminder of the power and fragility of democracy. We stand here, having delved into the life and experiences of an individual whose story became intertwined with a pivotal moment in American history - the January 6 attack on the U.S. Capitol by Trump supporters.

In the preceding chapters, we embarked on a voyage through Cassidy Hutchinson's life. We learned about her formative years and education in Chapter 1, discovering the seeds of curiosity and ambition that would propel her forward. In Chapter 2, we traced her remarkable journey from a humble internship to becoming a White House insider, a trajectory marked by determination and resilience.

Chapter 3 immersed us in the harrowing events of January 6, a day that will forever be etched in the annals of American history. We witnessed the shocking attack on the U.S. Capitol, an assault on the very heart of democracy that sent shockwaves across the nation and the world. It was a day that exposed deep divisions and tested the resilience of democratic institutions.

In Chapter 4, we delved into the details of the attack on the Capitol, seeking to understand the motivations and consequences of that dark day. We examined the stories of those who participated and the implications of their actions on the nation's political landscape.

Finally, in Chapter 5, we bore witness to Cassidy Hutchinson's courageous testimony before the January 6 Committee. Her words echoed through the halls of Capitol Hill, serving as a stark reminder of the importance of accountability and truth in the face of adversity.

As we reflect on this journey, we extend our deepest appreciation to you, our cherished readers. Your investment of time and resources in exploring this biography speaks to your commitment to understanding the complexities of the world we inhabit. In an age where information flows ceaselessly, your dedication to seeking knowledge is commendable.

This biography is a testament to the power of storytelling and the role it plays in shaping our understanding of the world. It is a reminder that history is not a static entity but a living, evolving narrative, influenced by the actions and choices of individuals like Cassidy Hutchinson.

We hope this journey has left you with a deeper understanding of the events of January 6 and the individuals who played pivotal roles on that fateful day. It is our fervent hope that this biography has provided insight, sparked curiosity, and encouraged reflection on the profound issues of our time.

In closing, we invite you to carry the lessons and stories within these pages forward as you engage with the world. Democracy, as we have seen, is a fragile experiment, one that requires our vigilance and active participation. It is through knowledge and understanding that we can navigate the complexities of our era and work toward a future marked by unity, accountability, and the unwavering pursuit of truth.

Thank you for sharing in this journey, and may the pages of this biography continue to inspire your quest for knowledge and understanding.

With deepest gratitude,

Timeless Talesmith.

Made in the USA
Columbia, SC
10 October 2023